The Consumer Guide To
FINDING FREE OR LOW COST
HEALTHCARE IN ARKANSAS

CONSUMER GUIDE TO FINDING FREE OR LOW COST HEALTHCARE IN ARKANSAS

Law Offices of Lisa Douglas, Inc.
2300 Main
North Little Rock, AR 72114
501-798-0004
www.LisaGDouglas.com

TABLE OF CONTENTS:

Foreword
WHY THIS BOOK?

I wrote this book to assist Social Security Applicants in finding medical treatment. In order to prove your disability, a claimant must have the adequate medical documentation to prove their claim. Without this necessary documentation, the claimant is not able to prove their claim. Many of the claimants do not have healthcare coverage and lack the funds to pay for any healthcare.

Because this healthcare and the documentation that results is so vital to your claim it is essential to receive this healthcare. If you are like most, this is the first time you have resorted to the system that you paid into and now lack the funds to prove up your case, because you cannot afford the healthcare. That is why I wrote this book, to equip you with the resources to pursue the healthcare and medical documentation to prove up your case.

I wrote this book for **you.** Hopefully you will find it a valuable tool that will give you some valuable information to consider while you are seeking healthcare.

This book is too limited to explore every issue or address each possible question you may have.

Further, this book is not intended to give legal advice and nothing in this book is legal advice. Obtaining this book from me does not create an attorney client-relationship between us. I do not sign up everyone who calls my office that has a social security claim.

This book lists both federally funded health care centers and free to low cost clinics.

Federally-funded health centers care for you, even if you have no health insurance. You pay what you can afford, based on your income.

These federally funded health centers provide primary medical and dental care to people of all ages, whether or not they have health insurance.

The Health Resources and Services Administration (HRSA) is an agency within the U.S. Department of Health and Human Services. Millions of Americans receive affordable health care through HRSA programs.

These federally funded health Centers can be found at http://www.hrsa.gov and are designated by *astericks in this book.

Additional Free Clinics or Low Cost Clinics can be found at:
http://freeclinicdirectory.org/arkansas_care.html
These clinics are designated by + in this book.
Another online source to locate free clinics can be found at:
http://www.freemedicalsearch.org/sta/arkansas
or
www.freemedicalcamps.com
For more information on free clinics or to find out how you can help at a free clinic, go to http://www.freeclinics.us

County: Ashley County, AR

*MAINLINE HEALTH SYSTEM, INC.
233 N Main St
Portland, AR 71663-9230
Telephone Number: 870-737-2221
Appointment Number: 870-737-2737 x21

+FOUNTAIN HILL MAINLINE
127 N. Hickory St.
Fountain Hill, AR 71642
Number: 870-853-9993

*WILMOT CLINIC
203 McCombs
Wilmot, AR 71676-8800
Telephone Number: 870-473-2274
Appointment Number: 870-737-2737 x21

County: Benton County, AR

*COMMUNITY CLINIC ROGERS MEDICAL
1233 W Poplar St
Rogers, AR 72756-4245
Website: www.communityclinicnwa.org
Telephone Number: 479-636-9235
Appointment Number: 479-751-7417 x6069

*COMMUNITY CLINIC ROGERS/DENTAL
3710 Southern Hills Blvd
Rogers, AR 72758-8041
Website: www.communityclinicnwa.org
Telephone Number: 479-936-8600
Appointment Number: 479-751-7417 x6069

*COMMUNITY CLINIC SILOAM SPRINGS
MEDICAL
500 S Mount Olive St Ste 200
Siloam Springs, AR 72761-3602
Website: www.communityclinicnwa.org
Telephone Number: 479-524-9550
Appointment Number: 479-751-7417 x6069

+SAMARITAN HOUSE COMMUNITY CENTER
1211 W. Hudson Road
Rogers, AR 72756
Telephone Number: 479-636-4198

County: Boone County, AR

+THE MEDICAL CLINIC MISSION OF
HARRISON ARKANSAS
1400 South Pine Street
Harrison, AR 72601
Telephone Number: 870-365-0341

County: Calhoun County, AR

*CABUN RURAL HEALTH SERVICES, INC.
402 N Lee St
Hampton, AR 71744-8937
Website: cabun.org
Telephone Number: 870-798-4299
Appointment Number: 870-798-4064

County: Carroll County, AR

*BOSTON MOUNTAIN RURAL HEALTH
CENTER, INC.
1103 E Main St
Green Forest, AR 72638-2810
Website: bmrhc.org
Appointment Number: 870-448-3796

County: Chicot County, AR

*DERMOTT MEDICAL AND DENTAL CLINIC
300 S School St
Dermott, AR 71638-2127
Telephone Number: 870-538-3355
Appointment Number: 870-538-3355 x26

*EUDORA CLINIC
579 E Beouff St
Eudora, AR 71640-3090
Telephone Number: 870-355-2512
Appointment Number: 870-737-2737 x21

County: Clark County, AR

*AMITY COMMUNITY HEALTH CENTER
329 N Hill St
Amity, AR 71921-9635
Website: cabun.org
Telephone Number: 870-342-5606
Appointment Number: 870-798-4064

County: Clay County, AR
*CORNING AREA HEALTHCARE, INC.
1300 Creason Rd
Corning, AR 72422-1716
Telephone Number: 870-857-3399
Appointment Number: 870-857-3399 x222

County: Cleburne County, AR
*ARcare - 85
1511 Highway 25B
Heber Springs, AR 72543-1701
Website: www.arcare.net
Telephone Number: 501-362-9426
Appointment Number: 870-347-2534

+HEBER SPRINGS FAMILY HEALTH
CENTER
1716 West Searcy
Heber Springs, AR 72543
Telephone Number: 501-362-7595

+CHRISTIAN HEALTH CENTER
501 West Main
Heber Springs, AR 72543
Telephone Number: 501-362-2252

County: Cleveland County, AR

*RISON CLINIC
505 Sycamore
Rison, AR 71665
Telephone Number: 870-325-6255
Appointment Number: 870-543-2315

County: Craighead County, AR
*JONESBORO FAMILY HC - NORTH
1530 N Church St
Jonesboro, AR 72401-1515
Website: www.wrrhc-ar.org
Telephone Number: 870-802-3586
Appointment Number: 870-347-2534

*JONESBORO FAMILY HEALTH CENTER - SOUTH
2816 Fox Meadow Ln
Jonesboro, AR 72404-9346
Website: www.wrrhc-ar.org
Telephone Number: 870-347-2508
Appointment Number: 870-347-2534

*LAKE CITY HEALTH CENTER
1009 Highway 18
Lake City, AR 72437-9622
Website: www.wrrhc-ar.org
Telephone Number: 870-237-3399
Appointment Number: 870-347-2534
Appointment Number: 870-237-9928

County: Crawford County, AR

*MOUNTAINBURG FAMILY CLINIC
4 Highway 71 N
Mountainburg, AR 72946
Website: www.rvpcs.org/
Telephone Number: 479-369-2091
Appointment Number: 479-635-0091 x240

*MULBERRY FAMILY CLINIC
437 N Main St
Mulberry, AR 72947-8574
Telephone Number: 479-997-1484
Appointment Number: 479-635-0091 x240

County: Crittenden County,

*EAST ARKANSAS FAMILY HEALTH
CENTER, INC.
215 E Bond Ave
West Memphis, AR 72301-3550
Website: eafhc.org
Telephone Number: 870-735-3842
Appointment Number: 870-732-6520

County: Cross County, AR
*PARKIN MEDICAL CLINIC & PHARMACY
1740 Church St
Parkin, AR 72373
Website: www.wrrhc-ar.org
Telephone Number: 870-755-2234
Appointment Number: 870-347-2534

*WYNNE HEALTH CENTER
611 Julia Ave E
Wynne, AR 72396-3506
Website: www.wrrhc-ar.org
Telephone Number: 870-238-0377

County: Desha County, AR

UAMS
803 Highway 65 South
Dumas, AR 71639
Telephone Number: 870-382-2091

County: Drew County, AR

*MONTICELLO COMMUNITY HEALTH
CENTER
766 H L Ross Dr
Monticello, AR 71655-5706
Telephone Number: 870-737-2221
Appointment Number: 870-737-2222

County: Hempstead County, AR

*HOPE MIGRANT HEALTH CENTER
205 Smith Rd
Hope, AR 71801-8801
Website: cabun.org
Telephone Number: 870-777-8420
Appointment Number: 870-798-4064

County: Independence County, AR

*INDEPENDENCE FAMILY HEALTH
1183 Batesville Blvd
Batesville, AR 72501-8925
Website: www.wrrhc-ar.org
Telephone Number: 870-347-2534
Appointment Number: 870-347-2534

*INDEPENDENCE FAMILY HEALTH CENTER
1175 Vine St BPHC
Batesville, AR 72501-3526
Website: www.wrrhc-ar.org
Telephone Number: 870-251-9933
Appointment Number: 870-347-2534

County: Jackson County, AR

*NEWPORT MEDICAL CLINIC
1507 N Pecan St
Newport, AR 72112-2867
Website: www.arcare.net
Telephone Number: 870-523-2944
Appointment Number: 870-347-2534

*SWIFTON MEDICAL CLINIC
300 E Main St
Swifton, AR 72471
Website: www.wrrhc-ar.org
Telephone Number: 870-485-2234
Appointment Number: 870-347-2534

County: Jefferson County, AR

*ALTHEIMER CLINIC
309 S Edline
Altheimer, AR 72004-8559
Telephone Number: 870-766-8411
Appointment Number: 870-543-2315

*REDFIELD CLINIC
113 W River Rd
Redfield, AR 72132-9253
Telephone Number: 501-397-2261
Appointment Number: 870-543-2315

+JEFFERSON COMPREHENSIVE CARE SYSTEM
1101 Tennessee Street
Pine Bluff, AR 71601
Telephone Number: 870-543-2309
Telephone Number: 870-543-2380

County: Lafayette County, AR

*+LEWISVILLE FAMILY PRACTICE CTR.
1117 Chestnut St
Lewisville, AR 71845
Website: cabun.org
Telephone Number: 870-921-5781
Appointment Number: 870-798-4064

County: Lawrence County, AR

*COMMUNITY HEALTHCARE CENTER
3219 Highway 67B
Walnut Ridge, AR 72476-8567
Telephone Number: 870-886-5507
Appointment Number: 870-857-3399

County: Lee County, AR

*+LEE COUNTY COOPERATIVE CLINIC
530 Atkins Blvd
Marianna, AR 72360-2113
Telephone Number: 870-295-5225
Appointment Number: 870-295-5225

County: Logan County, AR

*+RIVER VALLEY PRIMARY CARE SERVICES INC.
9755 W State Highway 22
Ratcliff, AR 72951-9000
Website: www.rvpcs.org
Telephone Number: 479-635-5300 x240
Appointment Number: 479-635-0091

County: Lonoke County, AR

*ARCARE - 93
614 N Grant St BPHC
Cabot, AR 72023-2656
Website: www..arcare.net
Telephone Number: 870-347-2534
Appointment Number: 870-347-2534

*+CARLISLE MEDICAL CLINIC
821 East Park St Hwy 70
Carlisle, AR 72024
Website: www.wrrhc-ar.org
Telephone Number: 870-552-7303
Appointment Number: 870-347-2534

*ENGLAND HEALTH CENTER
227 Pine Bluff Hwy
England, AR 72046-2234
Website: www.arcare.net
Telephone Number: 501-842-3131
Appointment Number: 501-842-3131

County: Madison County, AR

***+BOSTON MOUNTAIN RURAL HEALTH
CENTER, INC.**
934 N Gaskill St
Huntsville, AR 72740-8903
Website: www.bmrhc.org
Telephone Number: 479-738-5500
Appointment Number: 870-448-3796

County: Mississippi County, AR

*HEALTHY PARTNERS
4102 Memorial Dr
Blytheville, AR 72315-5771
Website: eafhc.org
Telephone Number: 870-532-6001
Appointment Number: 870-732-6520

County: Monroe County, AR

*BRINKLEY HEALTH CENTER & PHARMACY
615 N Main St
Brinkley, AR 72021-2507
Website: www.wrrhc-ar.org
Telephone Number: 870-734-1150
Appointment Number: 870-347-2534

*+MID-DELTA HEALTH SYSTEMS, INC.
401 Midland St
Clarendon, AR 72029-2727
Telephone Number: 870-747-3381
Appointment Number: 870-747-3381 x226

+HOLLY GROVE HEALTH CENTER
106 South Smith Street
Holly Grove, AR 72069
Telephone Number: 870-462-3393

County: Montgomery County, AR

*MONTGOMERY COUNTY COMMUNITY
CLINIC
534 Luzerne St
Mount Ida, AR 71957-9449
Website: www.healthy-connections.org
Telephone Number: 870-867-4244 x118
Appointment Number: 479-394-2332 x500

County: Newton County, AR

*BOSTON MOUNTAIN RURAL HEALTH CTR
Hc 31 Box 310
Deer, AR 72628-9616
Website: www.bmrhc.org
Telephone Number: 870-428-5391
Appointment Number: 870-448-3796

County: Ouachita County, AR

*+BEARDEN HEALTH CENTER
2nd & School Street
Bearden, AR 71720
Website: cabun.org
Telephone Number: 870-687-3637
Appointment Number: 870-798-4064

County: Phillips County, AR

*LAKEVIEW AREA CLINIC
14264 Highway 44
Helena, AR 72342-9070
Telephone Number: 870-827-3201
Appointment Number: 870-295-5225

County: Poinsett County, AR

*+EAST ARKANSAS FAMILY HEALTH CTR
102 W Broad St
Lepanto, AR 72354-2200
Website: eafhc.org
Telephone Number: 870-475-2977
Appointment Number: 870-732-6520

*TRUMAN FAMILY HEALTH CENTER
417 W Main St
Trumann, AR 72472-3116
Telephone Number: 870-732-6520
Appointment Number: 870-732-6520

County: Polk County, AR

*WESTERN ARKANSAS TOTAL
COMMUNITY HEALTH CENTER (WATCH)
1201 Mena St
Mena, AR 71953-4280
Website: www.healthy-connections.org
Telephone Number: 479-437-3449
Appointment Number: 394-394-2332 x500

+HEALTHY CONNECTIONS
1310 Highway 71 North
Mena, AR 71953
Telephone Number: 479-243-0279

County: Prairie County, AR

*+DES ARC DENTAL CLINIC
405 Highway 11 N
Des Arc, AR 72040-3140
Website: www.wrrhc-ar.org
Telephone Number: 870-256-3009
Appointment Number: 870-347-2534

*+DES ARC HEALTH CENTER
405 Highway 11 N
Des Arc, AR 72040-3140
Website: www.wrrhc-ar.org
Telephone Number: 870-256-4178
Appointment Number: 870-347-2534

*+HAZEN MEDICAL CLINIC
100 E Front St
Hazen, AR 72064
Website: www.wrrhc-ar.org
Telephone Number: 870-255-3696
Appointment Number: 870-347-2534

County: Pulaski County, AR

*COLLEGE STATION CLINIC
4206 Frazier Pike
College Station, AR
Telephone Number: 501-490-2440
Appointment Number: 870-543-2315

*HOMELESS OPEN HANDS
1225 Dr Martin Luther King Dr
Little Rock, AR 72202-4743
Telephone Number: 501-244-2121
Appointment Number: 870-543-2315

*LITTLE ROCK CHC
1522 W 10th St
Little Rock, AR 72202-3526
Telephone Number: 501-376-1285
Appointment Number: 870-543-2315

+COMMUNITY HEALTH CENTERS OF
ARKANSAS
420 West 4th Street, Suite A
North Little Rock, AR 72114
Telephone Number: 501-374-8225

+CAMP ALDERSGATE
2000 Aldersgate Rd.
Little Rock, AR 72205
Telephone Number: 501-664-0340 ext. 356

+HARMONY HEALTH CLINIC
201 East Roosevelt
Little Rock, AR 72206
Telephone Number: 501-375-4400

County: Randolph County, AR

*+POCAHONTAS FAMILY MEDICAL CENTER
141 Betty Dr
Pocahontas, AR 72455-3602
Telephone Number: 870-892-9949
Appointment Number: 870-857-3399

County: St. Francis County, AR

*+HUGHES CLINIC
503 S Broadway St
Hughes, AR 72348-9701
Telephone Number: 870-339-4181
Appointment Number: 870-295-5225

County: Searcy County, AR

*+BOSTON MOUNTAIN RURAL HEALTH
CENTER
2263 Highway 65 N
Marshall, AR 72650
Website: www.bmrhc.org
Telephone Number: 870-448-5733
Appointment Number: 870-448-3796

County: Sebastian County, AR

*NORTH SIDE BEHAVIORAL HEALTH AND
SPECIALTY SERVICES
3202 N 6th St
Fort Smith, AR 72904-4164
Website: www.rvpcs.org
Telephone Number: 479-783-3900
Appointment Number: 479-635-4800

*RVPCS - NORTHSIDE CLINIC
4900 Kelley Hwy
Fort Smith, AR 72904-5000
Website: www.rvpcs.org
Telephone Number: 479-785-5700
Appointment Number: 479-635-5300 x240

+GOOD SAMARITAN CLINIC
615 North B Street
Fort Smith, AR 72901
Telephone Number: (479) 783-0233

County: Union County, AR
*+STRONG CLINIC
253 S Concord St
Strong, AR 71765
Website: cabun.org
Telephone Number: 870-797-7620
Appointment Number: 870-798-4064

County: Van Buren County, AR

*+BMRHC - CLINTON CLINIC
465 Medical Center Pkwy
Clinton, AR 72031
Website: www.bmrhc.org
Telephone Number: 501-745-7888
Appointment Number: 870-448-3796

*+BOSTON MOUNTAIN RURAL HEALTH CTR
110 Village Ln
Fairfield Bay, AR 72088
Website: www.bmrhc.org
Telephone Number: 501-884-6898
Appointment Number: 870-448-3796

County: Washington County, AR

*+COMMUNITY CLINIC SPRINGDALE
DENTAL
610 E Emma Ave
Springdale, AR 72764-4634
Website: www.communityclinicnwa.org
Telephone Number: 479-751-7417
Appointment Number: 479-751-7417 x6069

*+COMMUNITY CLINIC SPRINGDALE MEDICAL
614 E Emma Ave Ste 300
Springdale, AR 72764-4469
Website: www.communityclinicnwa.org
Telephone Number: 479-751-7417
Appointment Number: 479-751-7417 x6069

+NORTHWEST ARKANSAS FREE HEALTH CENTER
10 South College Avenue
Fayetteville, AR 72701
Telephone Number: 479-444-7548

+St. FRANCIS HOUSE NWA, INC.
614 E Emma Ave. #300
Springdale, AR 72764
Telephone Number: 479-751-7417

County: White County, AR

*ARcare - 14
2802 Highway 367 N
Bald Knob, AR 72010-3165
Website: www.arcare.net
Telephone Number: 870-724-6207
Appointment Number: 870-347-2534

*+BALD KNOB MEDICAL CLINIC
170 Highway 167 N
Bald Knob, AR 72010-4058
Website: www.wrrhc-ar.org
Telephone Number: 501-724-6207
Appointment Number: 870-347-2534

*SEARCY FAMILY HEALTH CENTER
406 Rodgers Dr
Searcy, AR 72143-7433
Website: www.wrrhc-ar.org
Telephone Number: 501-279-7878
Appointment Number: 870-347-2534

*+WHITE RIVER MED SERVICE CLINIC
606 W Wilbur Mills Ave
Kensett, AR 72082-9051
Website: www.wrrhc-ar.org
Telephone Number: 501-742-5697
Appointment Number: 870-347-2534

County: Woodruff County, AR

*+AUGUSTA DENTAL CLINIC
623 N 9th St
Augusta, AR 72006-2129
Website: www.wrrhc-ar.org
Telephone Number: 870-347-25 08
Appointment Number: 870-347-2534

*+COTTON PLANT MEDICAL CLINIC
125 Oak St
Cotton Plant, AR 72036
Website: www.wrrhc-ar.org
Telephone Number: 870-459-3588
Appointment Number: 870-347-2534

*MCCRORY HEALTH CENTER
801 N Edmonds
McCrory, AR 72101
Website: www.wrrhc-ar.org
Telephone Number: 870-731-5411
Appointment Number: 870-347-2534

*+WHITE RIVER RURAL HEALTH CENTER, INC.
623 N 9th St
Augusta, AR 72006-2129
Website: www.wrrhc-ar.org
Telephone Number: 870-347-2534
Appointment Number: 870-347-2508

*WHITE RIVER RURAL HEALTH WELLNESS
904 N 4th St
Augusta, AR 72006-2039
Website: www.wrrhc-ar.org
Telephone Number: 870-347-1137
Appointment Number: 870-347-2534

DISCLAIMER

This Book is Not Legal Advice. This information is general in nature and should not be relied on as a substitute for legal advice. This book is provided as an education service by Law Offices of Lisa Douglas.

These clinics are in no way affiliated with Law Offices of Lisa Douglas, Inc. These clinics may have changed their status since the printing of this book. It is recommended you call these clinics in advance to determine their status before relying upon this book.

www.ingramcontent.com/pod-product-compliance
Lightning Source LLC
Chambersburg PA
CBHW051303170526
45165CB00004B/1830